cabbage and whiskey

cabbage and whiskey

norman minnick

KINCHAFOONEE
CREEK PRESS ≈ ATHENS, GA

Kinchafoonee Creek Press
585 White Circle #29
Athens, Georgia 30605

www.kcpress.org

ISBN: 979-8-218-61528-4

CONTENTS

For Pablo

Good worts! good cabbage. Slender, I broke your head: what matter have you against me?

— Sir John Falstaff

i am not the whiskey you want

— Rupi Kaur

NEW
POEMS

CARNIVOROUS VULGARIS, *or* AMUSING INJURIES

Being a child of the seventies
I have a fear, which some consider
irrational, of being crushed
by a falling anvil or grand piano
or of running along and realizing
there is no ground beneath me.

GRAVITY

When we learned
about the earth in orbit
and began to feel ourselves

standing sideways, our
burdens became lighter.
Then some prankster

decided to turn the whole
goddamn thing upside
down so that we were

right side up. The sun rose
and set and the moon
followed suit. Time went

on and we grew old
and counted our scars while
our weight on this world

became too much to bear.
Then we noticed our sagging
breasts, our flaccid pensées...

ICH MÖCHTE EINE ANDERE HABEN

I went to Disney World one year.
You are right; it's not a very happy place... that is
until I discovered Epcot and fell in love
with this lovely German woman, Annika, serving
German bier at the bar in "Germany."
Ah, Annika, in a dirndl and braided pigtails,
who could have been eighteen or thirty-eight.
As long as I kept ordering drinks and handing her tips
she would fill me with promises
to whisk me away to Germany with her
once her summer internship was over.
So, I ordered another.

CAST AWAY

I woke up on a beach unsure how I got there.
"Fool," I said, "You've done it again! Walked out
on a perfectly good life. You probably had a loving wife
and well-behaved children. You probably had a dog
and a pension and a closet full of sweaters.
You probably had a Buick."

NAMASTE

I showed up for my first class at the Y
and placed myself at the back of the room.
The instructor introduced herself
explaining how yoga fosters inner awareness, focus,
and something about flexibility and self-confidence.
Then she noticed I was the only male in group.
She stated that if any men were here
to pick up women, this was not the class
for them. As laughter morphed
into hip circles and shoulder stretches, I rolled up
my mat and slunk out of the room.
On my way to the car, I saw
through the window a room of bodies
twisted into oddly convoluted knots.

THE NUN IN A WHEELCHAIR

She pushes the little lever forward and moves forward.
She pushes the little lever to the left and turns left.
She pushes the little lever to the right and turns right.
She pushes the little lever backward and moves backward.
She pushes the little lever back and forth
Back and forth, back and forth, back and forth,
And suddenly she stiffens, stares heavenward, and shouts
 "Ecce venio!"

INTEL

She came into the room where I was feigning sleep
and tried to seduce me. I have a confession to make
I said laying my head upon her breast. I do not
work for the CIA and I'm not on a secret mission
to gather intel for the United States government.
Her chest rose and sank. I'm listening... she said.

ROLL IN THE HAY

Initially I thought she must be kidding
when she asked if I'd like a roll in the hay.
My consent came most expeditiously
and yet I demurred, for I was curious. "Why
the archaic phrase, the oldfangled idiom,
the anachronistic cliché? I find your crude
use of euphemism quite alluring," I told her,
"But why such an old chestnut, obsolescent
innuendo, naughty illocution?"
She slapped me across the face.
"What kind of woman do you think I am!"

HELL BENT

I prefer leather
because like fine whiskey,
the more you abuse it
the more it improves.

GRAND THEFT AUTO

"Son, when I was your age..."
"I know, I know; you had to walk to school uphill both ways."
"I saved my quarters and stood in line
 at the arcade on Saturdays to play a game
 where I had to maneuver a frog across a busy street
 without being squashed. You spend all your time
 playing a game where you can buy a prostitute..."
"You're such a boomer, Dad. I never pay for prostitutes.
 They're called hookers, by the way.
 And I don't actually pay for them; I kill them
 when I am finished, I take the money back."

BOMB POPS

The kids across the street have had too much sugar again.
The boy is terrorizing his younger sister. Her screams
drown out the repeated jingle of Pop Goes the Weasel
from the ice cream truck that creeps down the street.
He chases her with something probably dead that he found
in the yard, while three siblings sit on the porch and watch,
popsicle juice dribbling down their shirts. It's starting
to get out of hand. Their mother comes outside in a robe
and scolds them with a slew of ultimatums.
They ignore her. They ignore her. They ignore her.
She appears to be well into her third trimester.

WORK

On the job site I pretend
I can't get the gizmo to work
so I call Susan over because
I've been wanting to work
more closely with her
and because she has such
delicate hands. She brings
an umbrella even though
it's not raining and, besides,
we are indoors.
"Dance," she tells me,
so I do my best
Gene Kelly impersonation
and start to sing.
"Just don't sing," she says.
I love the way she admonishes me
and I blush a little.
"Here. All you had to do
was turn it off and turn it
back on," she says
handing me the gizmo
warm from being
in her soft hands.

SELLING FRAGRANCES

Ocean Drive, Miami Beach. She is selling
fragrances. Ylang-ylang, Patchouli, Rose Geranium,

Mint, fine replicas of Yves Saint Laurent, Drakkar,
Eternity. She must have come from the sea. Her

sun-freckled breasts pushed up and swelling
like ocean waves at midday. She sees my eyes darting

like a panicked fish from her eyes to her breasts
and back again to her eyes and back again to her breasts

then back again to her eyes, which are as dark
as the sea at night. Her lips are like the inside

of a conch shell, not in color, but in smoothness —
this is her game, by the way — and secrecy.

She knows that when she tells me her name, a name
I'll not remember, and moves closer, her breasts

threatening to press against my chest, that
any amount of reasoning in me will set sail.

I know this too; am all too aware, yet complicit
in the transaction of not-so-secret trade secrets.

I want only one thing this singular moment
and, poor sailor that I am, purchase another.

DRIVING AROUND

I drive across town to the Family Dollar
for a particular notebook that fits neatly
on my right thigh. This allows me to write
as I drive. Today my thoughts were racing
too fast. I was weaving into other lanes
and ignoring stop signs, so I pulled
into a KFC parking lot
and let the engine idle as Bob from Iowa,
long-time listener, first-time caller,
complained about immigrants
crossing the border.
                As I turned the page
to jot down my next poetic coup
a man rushed up to my car
pushed through the open window
a paper bag of deep-fried smells
and told me in a thick accent
to have a nice day and drive safe.

HAPPINESS CAN BE CURED

1

A band of mall walkers
with matching strides
and coordinated sweat suits
traces the perimeter of the floorplan
to prolong their remaining days.

2

What are they so happy about?

3

Tony Hoagland died. I found out
by text as I was eating lunch
at the food court in a suburban
shopping mall. Am I, like everyone
else, subject to cliché? Is this simply
coincidence, he being the poet-laureate
of food courts? Or am I being mocked
by the fates who plot such things?

4

He died and I dine alone
among a cast of zombies
consumed by smartphones
while children scream with laughter
chasing one another around
polyurethane toadstools
in a semi-enclosed playground.
As I guide Kung Pao chicken
into my mouth with a plastic fork,
I hear an adult say to a child
to turn her frown upside down
and I feel for the kid.

5

Sometimes we must savor
our unhappiness, bathe in it.
I wish everyone would stop telling me
to smile. I want to say to everyone,
as Tony said to us once when we had
to say goodbye: "fuck you
and all your happiness."

6

The mall walkers are back,
smiling as if their lives depend on it.
They never spend money. And they never
get chased by a security guard on a Segway

like the teenagers who parade
the same perimeter on Saturday nights
showing off with skintight jeans and nose rings.

7

I first read Tony Hoagland in a booth
of Le Tub Saloon in Hollywood, Florida
where my buddies and I would gather
for burgers and beer. Jay handed me a copy
of *Donkey Gospel* and said, "You've got
to read this guy," which, I suppose,
is how Tony's poetry is often introduced.

8

Now I eat alone in a well-lit public place.
I write happiness can be cured
on the back of a food-stained receipt,
smile at my cleverness and fold it
neatly into my wallet
for safe keeping.

CELEBRATION OF LIFE

My father said he doesn't want us
to have a celebration of life after he has died.
He wants us to celebrate his life while he's still alive.

So, we do. And, boy, do we celebrate!

Every weekend is filled with song and dance
and balloons and confetti and streamers aplenty.
And it's all for him for being alive.

Sometimes he needs a little respite from the noise
and slips out the back, and we don't even realize
until the party is over that he is gone.

from

THE
OVERREACHER

NEVER-NEVER LAND, *sometimes called*
THE BRIDE OF CONCUPISCENCE, *or*
HAPPILY EVER AFTER

As the groom slides the garter
off the leg of his pale, pristine
bride, he gazes into the eyes
of a primed bridesmaid.

A tiny tuxedo of a boy is blessed
with the fruits of youthfulness
as he catches an eyeful
of the bride's dark phenomenon.

THE PURCHASE

I found William
Carlos Williams

in a suburban
shopping mall

something
there is

not right
in that

ETC. ETC.

Everybody has a patois
or a gunshot wound or has
simply overdosed on heroin.

LONE RANGER HERO POET

No one knows where a hero gets his hero ways.
This lone ranger is such today
as he rears back in his saddle to kiss farewell
his mother and sends her back to her den with a sonly yeehaw.
He blazes a new trail to the great beyond
stopped by his own flesh and blood, (no one
knows it yet, though everyone suspects it)
the bringer of bad news, who sets the ranger back on his high
    throne
to ride once again and write it down this time!

Our hero saunters along hands stretching his pockets
sopping up after himself and others like him while
damsels in drag point and laugh. Overhead naked metal birds fly
toting hundreds of medievals who are nourished on kissy movies,
salted peanuts and soda pop.

Shaking his fist at the sky
the lone ranger hero poet cries out,
Before there were streets there was never poetry like this!

I FORGOT MYSELF

In my day I went out
to meet some zealous drinking buddies.

I feel I may have dis
engaged myself from them

by walking out to them
on the water.

from

TO TASTE
THE WATER

MIGRATION

The sun has nothing left to say.
The grass breathes a slow sigh of relief.
All day I have been raking leaves.
Now, as evening approaches, my attention
is called to the sky. Geese
call to one another across their perfect form.
The last one turns its head and looks at me. It wonders
how I live my life and neither lead nor follow.

THE CURRENT

for Stanley Kunitz on his 100th birthday

At first I thought to pick up the phone
and call you. But you don't know me.
So I took your book,
snuck out of the office, and sat on the grass
in the shadow of a white ash
beside this derelict canal.

Built in the 1830s
it was supposed to connect
the Wabash Canal with the Erie Canal.
Then the railroads came.

After reading aloud
a few of my favorite poems,
I looked into the water.

A bluegill swam against the current, turned
perpendicular to the shore
and allowed the current
to push it back to where it began.

It did this over and over again.

It must have been at play.
What else could it do?

HANDS

I have stood close to death
and still don't know what to do with my hands
at a crowded funeral.

They give comfort
to the darkness inside pockets

but swim frantically
when someone places their hand on my shoulder
and turns me toward the door.

As the coffin is closed
a voice in cold air says
it is time to go.

WAITING ROOM

All around me people are dying.
An old tune set to Muzak
becomes the soundtrack
to our despair. Beside me,
an old woman,
her right hand spread
long and narrow on her husband's knee
like a speckled trout thrown from the river,
her left clutching a tissue in her lap.
She says to her husband, *I'll tell you*
when to worry. This comforts me
as I search for a better life
in a well-traveled magazine
trying not to look up,
trying not to touch
its wrinkled pages.

BAINBRIDGE, INDIANA

Sitting at the corner of Cherry and Main
in Bainbridge, Indiana, I hear the hum
of an ice machine beside the BP.

A hawk soars overhead, its right wing
missing a few feathers.

Someone has shot five holes in the stop sign,
missing all four letters.

A small, white house sits comfortably
on its half-acre, the windows open.
A curtain billows out from one.

There's no sound but the ice machine
and a few birds somewhere high in a tree.

THE BUSY STREET

Who is he walking alone
who claims to mind his own business
as the wind sweeps him along into another body —

an uncomfortable body with cold feet
and hands too dirty to shield his eyes
from flying debris?

Is he the boy who wanders off in class
and sits down to share his lunch with the pigeons?

Is he the nervous boy who loosens his tie to stand off-key
in the strange arena below Emily Dickinson's window?

Or is he the young man ready to step into the street
of rushing traffic, calling to a woman

who disappears behind a bus, moving?

POEM BETWEEN BASHO
AND LEVERTOV

Don't follow in the footsteps of the old poets,
seek what they sought.

She wants me to cut
straight through the middle of the apple
so she can see the star at its core.

This is the year the old ones,
the old great ones
leave us alone on the road...

WALKING ALONG THE EDGE OF THE WOODS AT DUSK MY DAUGHTER ASKS ABOUT GOD AGAIN

God is in everything, I tell her,
hoping the mystery and matter-of-factness
will give her something to think about.
Everything? Everything.
The clouds? The grass?
What about the dirt?
What about me? What about
you? And before I can answer
a great horned owl,
almost as tall as my daughter,
looks at us.
It extends its massive wings
and with one downward thrust
lifts its body
and disappears, leaving
a small lump of fur and broken bones
in the dark grass.

FALLING ASLEEP

The eyes know.
The heartbeat
slows. Thoughts blur
and limbs become
useless.

A beautiful stranger
crosses the dance floor
mysterious and graceful,
takes me by the arm
and whispers, *Don't worry,*
I'll lead.

THE SANDPIPER

The sandpiper
is always
on the move.
It's odd.
When the tide
brings the food in
it's funny how
the sandpiper
works so hard
for so little.
The sandpiper
doesn't complain
of back pain
or muscle cramps,
doesn't need
a lawyer.
What the sandpiper knows
that we don't know
is how
not to get wet.

HOW POETRY COMES TO ME

after Gary Snyder

Seek not, a voice says.

I open my eyes to total darkness
and for a moment forget where I am.

When the lamp is not there,
a tremor runs the length of my body.

Outside my tent
something moves, and I can't remember
whether to play dead
or make myself appear
as large as possible.

HER IMAGE

My daughter,
captivated
by her inverse image
in the curve of a spoon,
turns it over and back
and over again,
and back again,
her image
upside down,
right side up,
faster, as if she might
trick the spoon.

Eat, I tell her.

PAY ATTENTION

All my life I have been told
to pay attention, stop daydreaming,
pay attention, keep up, pay
attention, get to work. So much emphasis
on the word *pay*, now I am broke, my mind crowded
and noisy. Guests who were not invited
will not leave. I am interested in this word
attention.

I step outside for fresh air.
Moon and owl compete
for the highest branch of a sugar maple.

from THINGS THAT FLY

I wanted to find a poem in what's hidden.

Outside my window
a nest of robins,
mouths open
heads thrust to the sky.

Their mother arrived,
placed something still alive
at the backs of their throats.

That night
drifting in and out of delicious sleep,
the poem I could not write came to life
at the back of my throat
and by dawn had learned to fly.

AT THE MERCY OF THE UNFORGIVING

A great wind came and claimed everything.

I have stood in this doorway for years
looking upon its wake — amazed by what it took:

the car, the mailbox, the dog on his chain;
it came and took everything —

the neighbor, the neighbor's dog and the neighbor's tree,
the tree by my window and the owl who watched me howl in
    my sleep,

and all the birds in all the trees along the street. It took
    everything —
the road and the grass and the water from the spring,

the highway and the church and even the YMCA.

It was angry and came without warning —
took the seasons, the war, yesterday and tomorrow.

It came swiftly and took the clouds and the graves,
heaven and hell.

And sadness! It even took sadness!

But there was one thing left, clinging to the frame of the door, having nearly gone unnoticed:

a wet leaf like the small hand of a child.

from

FOLLY

THE CHILD NERO

for Adam Zagajewski

He looks, dare I say it,
sweet. A boy like any other
who would have enjoyed

baseball, had it been invented,
a few stolen cigarettes
in the bathroom between classes,

who would blush every time
his Latin teacher called him
Claudius or Caesar Augustus.

See how he nearly blushes now
in this gallery far from Rome,
this cherub, far from his new home

in the Louvre.
Look at his chubby cheeks
and those winglike ears.

See how he stands
indifferent in his long flowing toga
among these school children

in their starched blue uniforms
who are being told about
the man this boy would become,

murderer of his mother, half
of Rome burned, stabbing himself
in the heart while uttering

with his last breath, *Jupiter,*
what an artist perishes in me!
See how he pretends not to hear.

IN THE PARKING LOT
OF THE DRY CLEANERS

Three spaces over a woman has a man
pinned against the door of a candy apple red
1973 z28 Chevy Camaro
with white racing stripes, leather interior
and chrome mag wheels.
Their lips are locked. I can almost hear
over the thumping bass
the knocking of their teeth.
His grubby fingers hesitate
at the hem of her shirt like immigrants
waiting at the border, nervous, alert.
From where I sit I can see
the soft, golden hair of her lower back
as it follows the curve between two dimples,
the Dimples of Venus,
toward the forbidden shadow
just beginning to show
at the low beltline of her jeans.
My hand leaves the steering wheel
and finds the warmth swelling
between my legs and the spot of pre-cum
that has seeped through my pants.
My wife in the rearview mirror blurs
with each thump of the bass as she exits
the dry cleaners with my only suit
hanging like a minister inside a plastic sleeve.

AT THE AUTO REPAIR SHOP

Everything,
even the gumball machine, is grimy.
The mechanic has his name on a patch
above his heart. His fingernails
and the deep lines in his cracked hands
are forever black. The shop smells
like tires and stale coffee.
Chilton's service repair manuals
and parts catalogues are stacked
behind the counter. No one notices
the zweep zweep sound of an air
impact wrench torquing lug nuts.
Cigarette butts float in the toilet
above which hangs a pinup
showing a woman wearing only a pair
of bright red high heels
that compliment
the bright red muscle car
she sprawls over.
She has thick, dark pubic hair
which upon closer examination
is only the smudge
of a greasy thumbprint.

A WEEK WITHOUT POETRY

Sunday

I sit and stare at nothing. I am.
Listen to the children playing
down the street farther than they have
ever been without supervision.
Sit and wait. Listen. Besieged
by children. I am base.

Monday

I stand and think about not thinking.
This profane existence surrounded
by plastic spoons, Styrofoam cups,
beer bottles, chicken bones, old tires,
discarded Christmas trees, dirty diapers...

Tuesday

He stands like a dolt, a spineless
simpleton, a dumbass
with dandruff on his lapels,
holding his hat with both hands,
his coat is two sizes too big.
"Hey muttonchops, I'm talking to you,
you want a piece of me?"

Wednesday

An old lady in stone washed jeans
and a Harley Davidson T-shirt
climbs into the cab of a Peterbilt
her white perm done up like a cloud.

Thursday

Sitting like an odalisque on the love seat
reading *No Exit.* "Sartre," I say with a throat
full of phlegm. "Use a napkin," she says,
"for Chrissake wipe your face!"

Friday

A leather-skinned man with faded tattoos
holding onto the back of a garbage truck
flashes me a peace sign before hopping
down to collect my trash.

Saturday

I have fallen in love with a girl, insistent with freckles,
who carries a flat of azaleas across the street. She is in love
with something not me, evident by the angle of her chin.
Without a word I let her pass.

RILKE

The man beside me
pissing into the urinal trough,

his stream nearly crossing mine,
looks like Rilke

with his Fu Manchu moustache,
dark eyes and cleft chin.

Perhaps it is Rilke.
Perhaps my intention to move closer

to the ethereal, dream world
of my lyrical forefathers

has been lucrative. Perhaps
the great poet has come back

for one more surge of inspiration
that would lift him once

and for all off this earth.
He clears his throat, shakes

more than once, and leaves
without washing his hands.

AN OMELET

She orders an omelet for breakfast
with fresh herbs and goat cheese,
tells the waitress to please hold the peppers.

"Do you remember the first time you proposed to me?"
she asks as she cuts through the omelet
with the side of her fork.

I watch the melted cheese and uncooked egg
ooze between the tines and admire her concentration
on this simple procedure.

"You wouldn't touch your knee to the ground
because it was too muddy," she says, "Do you remember
how long I kept you waiting?"

THE OBOIST

I tell her how wonderful it is
to hear her play her oboe
on a fine day as this.

"It's a clarinet," she says.

Everything around us
alive, listening,
alert to our presence.

Her red hair
is pulled back tight
into a ponytail,
and her green eyes, her green
green eyes, hold me there.

And I, a brute animal
who has just learned to stand
on two legs,

can only grunt and sniff
and listen.

As she moistens her lower lip,
I lower my eyes, waiting

like the dark
instrument in her hands,
like the moment held
between us.

ANGEL MOUNDS STATE HISTORIC SITE

On the grounds
of the Middle
Mississippian

Indian village
near ceremonial
mounds, occupied

circa 1500 A.D.
near the Ohio River
in what is now

Southern Indiana,
a young boy
from the city

kicks a Pepsi machine
for not delivering
on its promise.

GOD AND TENNIS

He asked if he could share the bench
with me. His name is David Crawford
and he wanted to know what I was reading.
William Blake. Poetry. Do you get into
spiritual things, he asked. Sure, I replied,
still not seeing what was coming.
Do you mind if I share my beliefs with you,
and he continued with the usual – finding salvation
through Jesus Christ, the Bible as God's word,
and so on. I had looked hard
for a bench in a secluded area
with no luck and settled on this one
alongside the walking path
in the busiest section of the park. As he talked
I watched two teenage girls play tennis.
I asked him who he thought was better,
Venus or Serena Williams. He said
he doesn't follow tennis. He said he is a student
at The Southern Baptist Theological Seminary.
I asked who he thought God was talking to
when he said, "Let us make man
in our image." The thock, thock from the tennis court.
The laughter of children from the playground,
the squeal of a swing set.
He said it was Jesus and the Holy Spirit.
He wanted to talk about atonement.
I tried to engage him in a conversation
about metaphor when a tennis ball landed at his feet.
He looked at it as if he had never seen a tennis ball before
then chucked it back over the high fence.

COUNTRY MARK

On the porch of the Country Mark
pipe smoke, talk of rain.
Bob is scratching lottery
tickets again.

PHANTOM LIMB

Looking down upon the bay from this high ridge
I see kayakers, all pointing different directions.
They are learning the art of moving straight.

They say that when one loses a limb
he can still feel the presence of that limb,
an itch perhaps, or a caress on the hand.

Those below me have no clue
I am standing high above them.
Like their god, there is nothing I can do
to set them straight.

THE YOUNG GIRL

Three boys stand poolside and talk
in awkward syllabics to one
of two girls, trying not to let their voices
crack. She has an August tan in June,
is the prettier of the two,
and she knows it and regrets it
and answers each with terse replies
hoping they will go away and not
make her friend feel bad about herself.
Yet they don't take the hint
and continue to show themselves to her,
to tighten their stomachs and cross
their arms to show some kind
of definition in their chest and biceps.
Part of her enjoys the attention
and her friend knows it — the one
we've neglected to notice, the one
sitting beside her eating cheese puffs,
the tips of her fingers blazing like tiny
shriveled suns.

CARP FISHING IN AMERICA

We play their game and dig our heels
into the soft bank and reel them in to throw them back
and return home to make a fresh batch
of dough balls out of corn meal, molasses, a nip of Old Crow,
and other ingredients I promised not to reveal.
Arguably the ugliest creatures in the lake, carp are leviathans,
bottom dwellers, keepers of the underworld.
Bruisers of the murky water, they appear to us ancient,
heavy plated, with wide open mouths like vacuum
     attachments
and sinister barbs like handlebar moustaches.
Carp are fighters, barbaric and wicked. And in this way
they are proud and put up a good fight with more
     determination
than the toothy walleye or the lily-livered, yellow-bellied,
     pusillanimous bluegill.

BIPLANE

Right now a yellow
biplane is performing
aerobatic maneuvers
over my house. My wife
is in the other room
sweeping the floor.
She has her headphones on
and is singing "Tomorrow"
from "Annie." She sounds more
like a drunken Ms. Hannigan
than the kinky haired orphan.
I believe in prosperity, but have
no more means of supporting
my family than I did at twenty-one.
She is sweeping and I'm
writing poems about what to do
when it is summer
and you are unemployed.
Walk in the woods
at least once a day,
recite Yeats to the trees.
Take the kids to the pool.
Read fairy tales at night by flashlight.
Listen to Eddie Cleanhead Vinson
sing the blues on old scratchy records.
Attempt Bach on the cello.
Break out the old fishing poles.
Dig for night crawlers.
Walk to an abandoned pasture

at midnight and bathe in the sea
of fireflies. My trust in serendipity
has dissolved. I am catching up
on the classics: *Don Quixote,*
Moby Dick, Ulysses, Bleak House,
Lear. I already feel guilty
for not working and for
suggesting that my wife
can't sing. The yellow biplane
climbs up into the sky
then doubles back.
The pilot cuts the engine
and the plane falls straight
toward earth.

SUMMER NIGHTS

Under the trellis late into the night
we drank Wild Turkey and smoked pot
and insulted each other and pushed
each other around and cracked
jokes about each other's moms.
Someone was always
feeling up a girl in front of the others
while the rest pretended not to watch.
The moon was our chaperone.
A train passed each night.
I could hear it long before it came,
long after it had gone.

from

ADVICE FOR A YOUNG POET

PUBLISHING, THE
OLD-FASHIONED WAY

A gust of wind just blew open my folder. Now
my poems are scattered all over the neighborhood.
I see one way up in a tree and another
stuck to the windshield of a UPS truck.
The little girl down the street has picked one up
and is reading it. Now she's crying.

EASTER; OR, WHEN LILACS LAST IN THE PEE-STREAM BLOOM'D

Sitting outside in the warm sun drinking beer,
reading poetry, not thinking about Jesus. I am
alone and happy. The in-laws are inside discussing
their ailments. They think I will eventually come in
to pee, but there is a blooming lilac bush
that looks just fine to me.

THIS UGLINESS

New research shows
each of us emits
millions of bacteria
from our human
microbiomes to the air
that surrounds us

and that we each possess
a personal microbial cloud
like Pig-Pen from the Peanuts
comic strip. This is not

an aura, a field
of subtle, luminous
radiation that surrounds
a person, that holistic
healers and proponents
of parapsychology
claim to perceive.

Nor is it a metaphor
for repressed anxieties
or latent salacious desires
that would've had Freud
stroking his libido.

It's filth. Simply
filth. Poets, like myself,
with their Faustian bargain

have known this
since the beginning,
have been able
to perceive and embrace
this ugliness.

TAX SEASON

What I love about my wife
and myself when we are together
evenings in the living room, she
sitting beside her lamp, I beside
a glass of Kentucky's finest, the ice
clacking as it melts, the kids
tucked into bed, TV on
but neither of us paying
attention is that sometimes,
after long intervals,

we talk. Tonight it is about taxes —
not sex, which we refer to as "doing
our taxes," as in, "Hey, honey,
wanna go upstairs and work
on our taxes?" and which the kids
have already figured out. Now,
because they would stand on the
other side of the door and hear
the taxing grunted appeals
to a higher power
they wish to become accountants
when they grow up.

"We should get a refund
this year," she says as she thumbs
erratic patterns on the screen of her
device. I am thumbing through
a new anthology of "funny" poems
(says so right here on the cover)

snorting derision (she swears
I have allergies) with every turn
of the page. It reminds me of that fad
from the 90s when girls would wear
T-shirts with Sexy screen-printed
across the chest or sweatpants with
Bootylicious in a glittery script across
the bottom. If you have to advertise it,
it probably ain't true. Amiright? These
poems are by living or freshly deceased
poets and are extremely limited in their
range — mostly narrative, prose broken

into lines, which, I suppose, *is* the current
fashion. These poems also prove
Bill Knott's lugubrious bon mot that
there is an "epidemic of humorlessness"
in contemporary poetry. He is not included,
by the way. Neither is Dorothy Parker
or Alan Dugan or Wendy Cope or
Philip Larkin or Pound or Byron
or Dryden or Horace or Juvenal
or the Great Bard himself.

Nothing from *Spoon River*
or any of the poets in the *Greek Anthology*
who were and still are the funniest and most
honest of all poets in poetdom, such as
Marcus Argentarius, who was a contemporary
of Jesus of Nazareth, and wrote:
Hetero-sex is best for the man of a serious turn of mind,
But here's a hint, if you should fancy the other:
Turn Menophila round in bed, address her peachy behind,
And it's easy to pretend you're screwing her brother.

Pederasty was widespread in ancient Greece
as it has been in the Catholic church. Yet,
the Greeks had some good ideas, such as
democracy and eisphorá, or taxing the wealthy.
Plato and Diogenes "saw that the great
majority of the human species were reduced
to the situation of squalid ignorance
and moral imbecility, for the purpose
of purveying for the luxury of the few,
and contributing to the satisfaction
of their thirst for power." This quote
is from Percy Bysshe Shelley's essay
on Christianity. We need to pay attention
to this because it is apposite to our time.

I am not sure what apposite means, but
I do know that Shelley was one of our
greatest atheists and defenders of poetry
and of beauty. How ahead of their time
dead poets are! Yet, we allow them to lapse
into obscurity because of our vainglorious
obsession with all things trendy, inoffensive,
and breathing. This collection exposes
the fashion of poetry today that is beginning
to leave a brackish taste in my mouth,
and that I am myself exhibiting here,
and that is to call attention to the writing
as it happens. It is a holdover, and not
imitated well, of stream-of-consciousness
that Joyce and his coterie made fashionable.

There are a few good ones, of course:
John Berryman and Sharon Olds and
Frank O'Hara and Tony Hoagland

and Yusef Komunyakaa and Terrance Hayes
and Wanda Coleman...

Here I am doing another thing en flique:
name-dropping in hopes that my readers might
place me in congress with these card-carrying
and esteemed poets.

Maybe I am being too harsh
with the poetasters, their
pose-poems, and their conventions
of conventional nepotism.

Although I am a nice guy, I shoulder
envy. I can also be quite supercilious
because I read a good deal of classical
literature and I look with disdain upon those
who refuse to read the ones who came before
because they do not mention iPads
or Maxi Pads or Donald J. Trump
and are longer than one of his toilet tweets.

I also have little patience for hybrid forms
like the prose-poem (which is it?)
and those obnoxious abecedarians.
I am to the same extent quite impatient
with the School of Quietude, identity
politics, virtue signaling,
humorless PC liberals and
narrow-minded conservatives alike.

I am aware that my lines
are becoming narrower,
which makes me wonder

if I am losing steam
or if this is a manifestation

of my own narrowing
ambitions and hopes...

It's time for another pour
of bourbon. My wife, my
beloved, my forlorn lover
and only friend and I do not
dream aloud together anymore.

It's as if that were allowed only
in the early years of marriage
before children came along,
layers of debt complicated
tax statements, or when
soubriquets such as "Pudd'n"
and "Pet" took on different
meanings, and we had
a positive balance
in our checkbook.

TV DOES MAKE YOU LOOK FAT

The Meteorologist makes more money than I.
He tells me that Saturday will be partly cloudy
and that Sunday will be partly sunny.

When I call to ask the Meteorologist,
who makes more money than I,
where the sun will be on Saturday,

he asks how I got through to him.
He says the Meteorologist is not his real name
and that his family is out of town.

Before I can ask about Sunday,
he hangs up the phone, this,
the Meteorologist who makes more money than I.

THE HIGHLIGHT OF MY
TEACHING CAREER

Seventh graders reading out of old and tattered
textbooks I found at a Goodwill store (they had to share)

the ancient story of Orpheus and Eurydice,
who they were determined to pronounce *You're a dice.*

When she was abducted on her wedding day
there was a sense of agitation in the classroom, bodies

shifting in seats, the sound of gum snapping
between tongue and cheek, a lot of throat clearing.

A hand shot into the air, a question proposed. That ain't litichur!
Desks were thrown aside and two girls were on each other.

It looked like the ball of dust you see in a cartoon where
a hand sticks out one side and a foot sticks out the other,

except here were real yelps of pain, real names called,
real scratches of blood, real fistfuls of hair pulled.

No children were left behind in that mêlée.
Everyone got a good view. The students embraced

the common core of that canonical chant: *fight, fight, fight!*
This is the highlight of my teaching career, not because people
 got hurt

(they did), but because my principal was a former English
    teacher,
and on the incident report I got to explain, using my best
    grammar:

Two young ladies got into a debate over the question, Was
    You're a Dice
abducted before the vows or after. You see, they were fighting

over the curriculum, the subject matter! and this altercation
would go on my CV and look real good on a job application.

POSE POEM

This little block of prose puts on no pretense, although it does put on a post tense. It calls itself a poem while it is clearly not one of those. It postures as something it is not. Therefore, I shall call it a "pose poem." It employs short declarative and often incomplete sentences for reasons that are unclear. Like that kid in college who wore a boiler hat and carried around an empty pipe. He introduced himself as Howard J. McDowell, Esquire. Howie, as no one called him, also wore a waistcoat with a pocket watch accoutrement. He complimented this outfit with Chuck Taylor high tops for a sense of irony that no one understood. Did I mention there was no tobacco in his pipe?

THE TALK

Father walked in on me
my brain in one hand
my heart in the other

It'll do you no good
he said no good at all
once you realize that

you must learn
the difference between
need and desire, pleasure

and sacrifice and he
wept and I wept though
not for the same reasons

ADVICE FOR A YOUNG POET

Stop using the word cloaca. Use oubliette instead.
It's not the same, but it sounds better.

And stop using the word plethora. Try instead
putrefy, as in, "My love for you has putrefied."

Or, even better, pussyfoot, as in, "I am tired
of pussyfooting around the perfidies of our nuptials."

How about abomasum, apple-knocker, or pack mule
    (two words) as in,
"Bitch, I ain't your pack mule!"

Cold-blooded and honey-tongued are fairly obdurate.
They're from Shakespeare.

So is abstemious
but that's downright disgusting.

ACKNOWLEDGMENTS

Books

Advice for a Young Poet (chapbook). David Roberts Books,
    Cincinnati (2020)
Folly. Wind Publications, Nicholasville, Kentucky (2013)
To Taste the Water. Mid-List Press, First Series Award for
    Poetry, Minneapolis (2007)
The Overreacher (chapbook). Broadside Books, Indianapolis
    (1998)

Journals

Atticus Review: "Easter; or, When Lilacs Last in the Pee-Stream
    Bloom'd"
Azure: "Pose Poem"
Brazenhead Review: "Publishing, the Old-Fashioned Way"
Chelsea: "Things That Fly"
Chiron Review: "Never-Never Land"
Crab Orchard Review: "God and Tennis"
Defenestration: "The Nun in the Wheelchair"
Dirtcakes: "The Child Nero"
Exquisite Corpse: "The Sandpiper"
5x5: "Angel Mounds State Historic Site"
Flying Island: "The Purchase"
Folio: "Ich Möchte Eine Andere Haben"
Gadfly: "TV Does Make You Look Fat"
The Inflectionist Review: "The Talk"
Maize: "Hands"

Mangrove: "At the Mercy of the Unforgiving" (with the title "The Great Wind")

New World Writing Quarterly: "Carnivorous Vulgaris" (with the title "Amusing Injuries")

Notre Dame Review: "The Busy Street"

Oddball Magazine: "Intel"

The Oxford American: "At the Auto Repair Shop"

Poetry East: "Phantom Limb"

Poiesis: "The Oboist"

Southern Indiana Review: "In the Parking Lot of the Dry Cleaners"

Spillway: "The Highlight of My Teaching Career" and "How Poetry Comes to Me"

Split Lip: "Gravity"

Superpresent: "Intel"

The Texas Observer: "The Sandpiper"

Zone 3: "An Omelet"

Anthologies

"Biplane" appears in MOTIF *3: Work* from Motes Books, edited by Marianne Worthington.

"Etc. Etc." and "The Purchase" appears in *Bigger Than They Appear: Anthology of Very Short Poems* from Accent Publishing, edited by Katerina Stoykova-Klemer.

"God and Tennis" appears in *The Louisville Anthology* from Belt Publishing, edited by Erin Keane.

A NOTE ON THE TYPE

The text is set in Goudy Old Style, a classic old-style serif designed by Frederic W. Goudy, commissioned by American Type Founders and first released in 1915. Celebrated for its elegance and warmth, Goudy Old Style is characterized by its open counters, bracketed serifs, and slightly old-fashioned charm. Its graceful letterforms balance legibility with artistic flourish, making it a tasteful choice for poetry.

The titles are set in Mr Eaves, the sans-serif companion to Zuzana Licko's classic Mrs Eaves. Designed with matching weight, color, and proportion, Mr Eaves expresses his personality through a clean, geometric look, while preserving Mrs Eaves' signature elegance.

ABOUT THE POET

Norman "Buzz" Minnick is a poet and designer born and raised in Louisville, Kentucky.

According to the poet David Kirby, "Minnick's poetry says everything the collected works of Freud do but in so much less space and so beautifully. Using sharp-edged images with dazzling deftness, Minnick reminds us that there are terrors in the shadows and that kids of all ages are glad they're there."

Minnick is an unforgettable reader of his and others' poems, and as long as one of his children does not need him to jumpstart their car, he would be happy to come to your place and recite his poems or lead a writing workshop — for a small fee, of course. He has been known to work for pizza and beer in lieu of an honorarium.

He loves fried cabbage and bourbon whiskey.